Preschool Art

Drawing

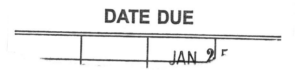
MaryAnn F. Kohl
Illustrations: Katheryn Davis

Dedication

Dedicated in memory of my grandmother, Mary Geanne Faubion Wilson,
the first published author I ever knew, who sparked my imagination
when she told me that angels made my freckles
when they kissed me on the nose as I slept.

Acknowledgments

I would like to thank my editor, Kathy Charner, for her humor and kindness
in our editor-author relationship. Sometimes I think we have too much fun to call this work!
In addition, I would like to thank the owners of Gryphon House, Leah and Larry Rood,
for their support and friendship, and their belief in this book and in me.
Most important, my thanks go to my husband, Michael,
and my daughters, Hannah and Megan, who keep my mind clear,
tell me when I've been wonderful or when I haven't and
remind me of what is most important in life.

Drawing

It's the process, not the product!

MaryAnn F. Kohl

 gryphon house®, inc.
Beltsville, Maryland

Library of Congress Cataloging-in-Publication Data

Kohl, MaryAnn F.,
    Preschool art: it's the process, not the product! / MaryAnn F. Kohl; [illustrations, Katheryn Davis].
        p.   cm.
    "A MaryAnn Kohl book."
    Inludes indexes.
    Contents: [1] Craft and construction --[2] Clay, dough, and sculpture -- [3] collage and paper -- [4] Painting -- [5] Drawing.
    ISBN 0-87659-223-X (v.5)
    1. Art--Study and teaching (Preschool)--Handbooks, manuals, etc. I. Title: craft and construction. II. Title: Clay, dough, and sculpture. III. Title: Collage and paper. IV. Title: Painting. V. Title: Drawing. VI. Davis, Katheryn. VII. Title.
LB1140.5.A7 K64 2001
372.5'044--dc21

2001018468

Illustrations: Katheryn Davis
Cover photograph: Straight Shots Product Photography, Ellicott City, Maryland.

Bulk purchase

Gryphon House books are available at special discount when purchased in bulk for special premiums and sales promotions as well as for fund-raising use. Special editions or book excerpts also can be created to specification. For details, contact the Director of Marketing at the address above.

Disclaimer

The publisher and the author cannot be held responsible for injury, mishap, or damages incurred during the use of or because of the activities in this book. The author recommends appropriate and reasonable supervision at all times based on the age and capability of each child.

Table of Contents

Introduction 6

Activities

Index 59

It's the Process, Not the Product

Why is art process important?

Young children do art for the experience, the exploration, and the experimentation. In the "process" of doing art, they discover creativity, mystery, joy, and frustration, which are all important pieces in the puzzle of learning. Whatever the resulting masterpiece—be it a bright, sticky glob or a gallery-worthy piece—it is only a result to the young child, not the reason for doing the art in the first place.

Art process allows children to explore, discover, and manipulate their worlds. Sometimes the process is sensory, such as feeling slippery cool paint on bare fingers. Other times it is the mystery of colors blending unexpectedly, or the surprise of seeing a realistic picture evolve from a random blob of paint. Art process can be a way to "get the wiggles out," or to smash a ball of clay instead of another child.

How can adults encourage the process of art?

Provide interesting materials. Stand back and watch. Offer help with unruly materials, but keep hands off children's work as much as possible. It's a good idea not to make samples for children to copy because this limits their possibilities.

Sometimes adults unknowingly communicate to a child that the product is the most important aspect of the child's art experience. The following comments and questions serve as examples of things to say that will help encourage each child to evaluate his or her own artwork:

Tell me about your artwork.

What part did you like the best?

I see you've used many colors!

Did you enjoy making this?

How did the paint feel?

The yellow is so bright next to the purple!

How did you make such a big design?

I see you made your own brown color. How did you do it?

Process art is a wonder to behold. Watch the children discover their unique capabilities and the joy of creating. This is where they begin to feel good about art and to believe that mistakes can be a stepping stone instead of a roadblock—in art as well as in other aspects of their lives. A concept children enjoy hearing is, "There's no right way, there's no wrong way, there's just your way."

Getting Ready!

Being prepared makes art experiences all the more enjoyable.
Here are some tips for success:

Covered Workspace

Cover the workspace—whether it is a table, floor, chair, wall, or countertop—with newspaper. Tape it down to prevent wiggles and spills of art materials. It's so much easier to bunch up sheets of paint-filled, sticky newspaper and find a clean space underneath than to clean up uncovered workspaces time and again. Other workspace coverings that work well are sheets of cardboard, an old shower curtain, a plastic table-cloth, big butcher paper, and roll ends of newsprint from the local newspaper print shop.

Handy Cleanup

Make cleanup easy and independent for young artists. All the less worry for the adult in charge! Place a wet sponge or pads of damp paper towels next to the art project for a simple way to wipe fingers as needed. Rather than have children running to the sink, fill a bucket with warm soapy water and place it next to the work area. Then add a few old towels for drying hands. Damp rags and sponges are handy for wiping spills, tidying up, and cleaning splatters as needed.

The Cover-up

An old apron, Dad's old shirt (sleeves cut off), a smock, and a paint shirt are all helpful cover-ups for creative preschoolers. Instead, consider this: wear old play clothes and old shoes and call them "art clothes," used for art only. It's a wonderful feeling to get into art without being concerned about protecting clothing. These clothes become more unique with time and are often a source of pride!

Other Tips

- Create a separate drying area covered with newspapers. Allow wet projects to dry completely.
- Always protect a larger circle of space than the immediate area around the project. Think about floors, walls, and carpets (maybe even ceilings!).
- Shallow containers are often mentioned in the Materials lists. These include cookie sheets, flat baking pans, clean kitty litter trays, plastic cafeteria trays, painter's pans, and flat dishes and plates.
- It's never too late to start collecting recyclables for art. Save collage materials, fabric and paper scraps, Styrofoam grocery trays, yarn, sewing trims, and even junk mail.
- Wash hands thoroughly before starting any edible activity.
- Do activities inside or out unless specifically noted as an outdoor activity only.

Using the Icons

Each page has icons that help make the projects in Drawing more useable and accessible. The icons are suggestions only. Experiment with the materials, vary the suggested techniques, and modify the projects to suit the needs and abilities of each child.

Age

The age icon indicates the general age range of when a child can create and explore independently without much adult assistance. The "& Up" means that older children will enjoy the project, and that younger children might need more assistance. Children do not always fit the standard developmental expectations of a particular age, so decide which projects suit individual children and their abilities and needs.

Planning and Preparation

The plan and prep icon indicates the degree of planning or preparation time an adult will need to collect materials, set up the activity, and supervise the activity. Icons shown indicate planning that is easy or short, medium or moderate, or long and more involved.

Help

The help icon indicates the child may need extra assistance with certain steps during the activity from an adult or even from another child.

Caution

The caution icon appears for activities requiring materials that may be sharp, hot, or electrical in nature. These activities require extra supervision and care.

Edible

Indicates activities that are safe to eat.

Hints

Hints are suggestions for the adults working with the artists.

Free Drawing

Materials

paper in a variety of textures, colors, and sizes
table, easel, or floor
crayons

Art Process

1. Place a piece of paper on a table, floor, or easel.
2. Draw freely on the paper. Use big, circular arm motions or small hand movements.
3. Experiment using different types of paper.

Variations

- Listen to music and color to the rhythm.
- Describe your drawing and ask an adult to write your description on the drawing or on a strip of paper that you can attach to it. (Most art professionals feel it is best not to write directly on the artwork unless the artist specifically wishes it to be placed there.)
- Use other drawing tools such as charcoal, regular or colored pencils, fine- or wide-point markers, pastels, chalk, or fabric pens.

Hints

- Tape the paper to the table to reduce tearing by enthusiastic artists.
- The possibilities of Free Drawing are endless and varied. Encourage artists to use their imagination!

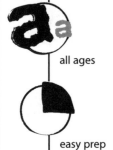

all ages

easy prep

Mark Making

Art Process

1. Place a sheet of paper or other material on the work surface.
2. Select a drawing tool and make marks on the paper.
3. Explore and experiment making designs using different drawing and design tools.

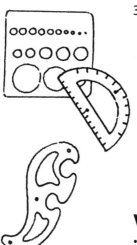

Materials

paper or other material on which to make marks
drawing tools (see list)
design tools (see list)

Drawing Tools

pencils
chalk
crayons
markers
pastels

Design Tools

ruler
protector
stencils
templates
lids
traceable objects

Variations

- The possibilities for this project are endless.
- Dip the design tools into paint and then make designs on the paper. Make marks in the sand or dirt, such as footprints or handprints. Trace the lids of jars and overlap the circle shapes. Use chalk and a ruler to measure lines.

Hint

- The key to developing creative imaginations is to stand back and let the artists make their own discoveries. The idea is to simply provide a variety of markers and design tools and let the artists explore and create.

Crayon Rubbing

Materials

textured objects (see list)
butcher paper or construction
    paper
tape
large crayons

Art Process

1. Place one or more textured objects under a piece of paper.
2. Tape the corners of the paper to the work surface.
3. Peel the paper off the crayons.
4. Holding the paper down with one hand, use your other hand to gently rub the flat side of a crayon over the covered objects.
5. Rub the paper until you have an imprint of the covered object.

Hint

- Age and experience will affect the final outcome of the Crayon Rubbing. Younger children will achieve varying degrees of quality with their rubbings.

Textured Objects

yarn
sandpaper
leaves
shapes cut or torn
   from heavy paper
scraps of fabric glued
   to cards

all ages

easy prep

More Rub-a-Rub

Art Process

1. Tape a sheet of paper over a textured work surface or material (see lists).
2. Peel the paper off the crayons.
3. Hold a crayon on its side and rub it over the paper.
4. Make rubbings of other surfaces and materials.

Materials

tape
large paper
textured work surfaces (see list)
textured materials (see list)
large crayons

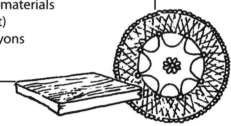

Variation

• Place the paper over various textures to "color in" a picture. For example, rub crayons over buttons to make eyes, flecked wallpaper to make clothing, and tree bark to make hair.

Textured Work Surfaces

wood grain
tree bark
concrete
walls
bricks
tiles
leather
signs with raised or recessed letters

Textured Materials

bumpy greeting cards
coins
license plates
corrugated cardboard
lace doilies
comb
piece of screen

Chalk Drawing

all ages

easy prep

help needed

Materials
poster chalk or pastels, variety of colors
paper
hair spray, optional

Art Process
1. Draw on a piece of paper using colored chalk or pastels.
2. When you finish the drawing, take it outside and spray it with hair spray to "set" the chalk (adult only). This will help prevent some of the smudging.

Hint
- Chalk is beautiful, but it smudges. Allow artists to experiment with the chalk and don't be too concerned with its inherent messiness. Children need to learn the qualities of chalk; smudging is one of them.

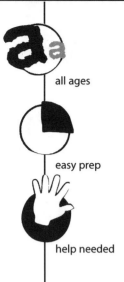

all ages

easy prep

help needed

Wet Chalk Drawing

SOAK CHALK
OVERNIGHT....

Materials

sugar
water
measuring cups
container
poster chalk
paper
hair spray, optional

Art Process

1. Mix ⅓ cup (80 g) sugar and 1 cup (240 ml) water in a container.
2. Soak the poster chalk overnight in the sugar solution. (Sugar water helps brighten the chalk colors and will stop some of the smearing.)
3. Draw with the wet chalk on a piece of paper.
4. When the artwork is dry, take it outside and spray it with hair spray to "set" the chalk and lessen the smearing, if desired (adult only).

Variation

- Instead of soaking the chalk overnight, dip the ends of dry chalk into the sugar solution.

Hint

- Keep in mind that although chalk breaks easily and smears, it has some unique qualities. You can brush it with a cotton ball, cotton swab, or tissue; blend it; use it brightly or lightly; crush it and use it as a powder; and mix powdered chalk to make new colors. It is messy and beautiful.

Dry Chalk, Wet Paper

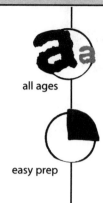

all ages

easy prep

Materials
water
dishpan
assorted paper
poster chalk or pastels

Art Process
1. Pour about 4" (10 cm) of water into a dishpan.
2. Dip a piece of paper into the water, thoroughly coating it.
3. Place the wet paper on a dry table and draw on it with chalk.
4. Experiment using different textures and types of paper.
5. Allow the artwork to dry for one or two days.

Variations
- Experiment by dipping a paintbrush into water and painting a design on dry paper. Then, use chalk to draw on top of the watery design.
- Try rubbing the chalk drawing with a cotton ball or tissue to smudge, blend, or smear it.

Hints
- On wet paper, chalk behaves somewhat like paint; it can be blended or smeared.
- Sometimes it helps to break large pieces of chalk in half or into smaller pieces for younger artists.

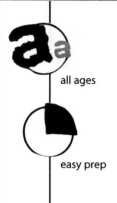

all ages

easy prep

Chalk and Liquid Starch

Art Process

1. Pour liquid starch into a small container.
2. Dip a paintbrush into the starch and paint on a piece of paper.
3. Use chalk to draw over the starch-covered paper. The liquid starch will brighten the chalk colors and help reduce the powdery smudging.

Variation

- Dip the end of the chalk directly into the starch and draw on the paper.

Hint

- Save the liquid starch and reuse it for other projects.

Sand and Glue Drawing

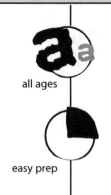
Materials

sand
large, wide tub
paper, poster board,
    or matte board
white glue in
    bottles

PLACE YOUR PAPER
ON THE SURFACE OF
THE SAND....

Art Process

1. Pour sand into a large, wide tub.
2. Place a piece of paper, poster board, or matte board on top of the sand.
3. Draw a design on the paper using the bottle of glue.
4. When you finish the design, scoop up handfuls of sand from the tub and cover the paper with it.
5. Lift a corner of the paper to let the excess sand fall back into the tub.

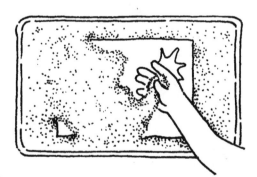

Variations

• Make colored sand. Mix sand and powdered tempera paint in an empty yogurt cup. Make several colors in different cups. Sprinkle bits of colored sand on specific areas of the design.
• Make sand drawings on the playground or sidewalk. Pour dry sand into an empty mustard squeeze bottle and make lines, dots, and other designs directly on the sidewalk. (Do not use glue.) Sweep away the sand when you finish.

Hints

• If the glue isn't available in bottles, pour white glue into cups and use paintbrushes or cotton swabs to apply it.
• A sand table also works well for this project.
• Purchase clean sand from a hardware store.
• If blobs of glue-sand fall off the paper into the tub, wait until they dry and remove them when they harden.

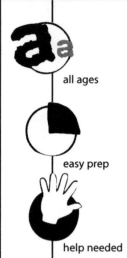

all ages

easy prep

help needed

Body Trace

Art Process

1. Place a large piece of butcher paper on the floor.
2. Lie down on the paper and spread your arms and legs a bit (to make tracing them easier).
3. Ask a second person to trace your body including fingers, hair, and other details.
4. When the tracing is complete, enhance your Body Trace using paints, crayons, markers, or fabric scraps and glue. The object is to add all of your physical features.
5. Cut out the shape and tape it to the wall (with the feet touching the ground and the head at your height).

Materials

large butcher paper
crayon or felt pen
paints and brushes, optional
fabric scraps and glue, optional
scissors
tape

Variations

- Make a Body Trace of your silhouette using black paper and white chalk.
- Decorate your Body Trace to look different from you, such as a being from outer space, a mother, a baker, or another character.

Hint

- Sometimes young artists are surprised and even disappointed with the tracing done by another person. You may wish to ask teenagers, parents, or other grown-up volunteers to do the tracing rather than other young artists.

Warm Crayon

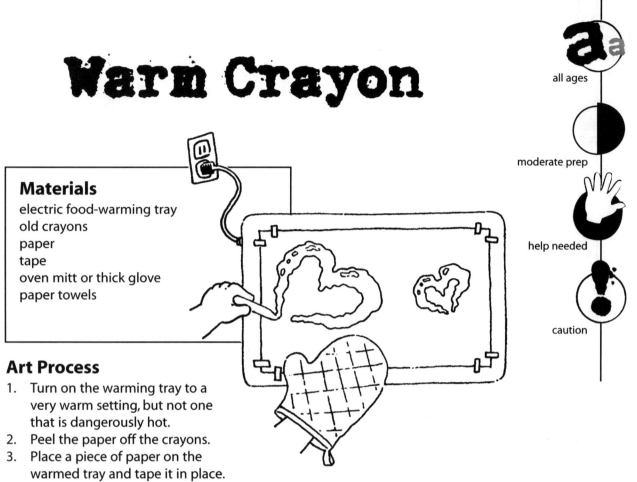

all ages

moderate prep

help needed

caution

Materials
electric food-warming tray
old crayons
paper
tape
oven mitt or thick glove
paper towels

Art Process
1. Turn on the warming tray to a very warm setting, but not one that is dangerously hot.
2. Peel the paper off the crayons.
3. Place a piece of paper on the warmed tray and tape it in place.
4. Put a thick glove or oven mitt on your non-drawing hand. Use this hand to hold the paper still.
5. With your other hand, move a peeled crayon slowly over the heated paper to make a melted design.
6. Wipe off the warming tray with a dry paper towel after each use.

Variation
• Cover the warming tray with heavy-duty aluminum foil and draw directly on the foil. Then, press a paper towel or piece of paper onto the melted design, peel the paper off, and the design will be transferred to the paper.

Hints
• Search garage sales and thrift stores for a food-warming tray.
• Make sure the artists keep their hands and arms off the warming tray.
• Tape the electric cord to the table with masking tape.
• Supervise this project closely.

all ages

moderate prep

help needed

caution

Iron Wax Paper

Art Process

1. Place a thick pad of newspaper on the work surface.
2. Cut the wax paper into 8" x 10" (20 cm x 25 cm) pieces. Place a sheet of wax paper on the newspaper.
3. Peel the paper off the crayons. Grate the crayons over the sheet of wax paper.
4. Place a second sheet of wax paper over the crayon shavings.
5. Cover the wax paper with a sheet of newspaper.
6. Set the iron to "warm" and iron over the newspaper. This will melt the crayon shavings and "glue" together the pieces of wax paper.
7. Remove the top sheet of newspaper.
8. Trim the excess edges of the wax paper.
9. If desired, glue a piece of yarn to the project and hang it in a window.

Variations

- Use a variety of shapes and sizes of wax paper.
- Frame the finished project with colored paper.
- Instead of rubbing the iron back and forth, press it straight down and lift it straight up to create a different design in the melted crayon.

Hints

- Most children can be very careful. With careful supervision, the artists can do the ironing themselves.
- Tape the iron cord in place so artists don't trip over it.
- Supervise this project at all times.

Handful Scribble

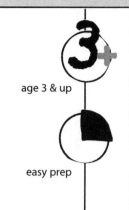
Materials

masking tape
paper
crayons, all the same length
rubber band
music, optional

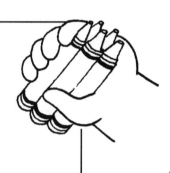

Art Process

1. Tape a piece of paper to the work table.
2. Gather a handful of crayons (three or more).
3. Tap the bundle of crayons against the paper to make sure all the crayon points are even.
4. Wrap the bundle with a rubber band.
5. Scribble and color on the paper using the crayon bundle. The crayons will make a rainbow-like design.
6. If desired, listen to music and color to the rhythm.
7. Remove the tape, turn the paper over, and scribble some more.

Variations

- Paint over the design with a wash of blue, black, or purple paint to make a crayon resist.
- Use the artwork for wrapping paper, or as a background for a framed picture or finger painting.

Hint

- Music makes some artists very energetic. Use large paper to accommodate "dancing arms."

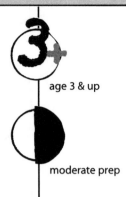

age 3 & up

moderate prep

Paint Crayons

Materials
water
cup or small dish
*paint crayons
paper
paintbrushes,
 optional

Art Process
1. Pour water into a cup or small dish.
2. Dip a paint crayon into the water.
3. Draw on a piece of paper with the moistened paint crayon.
4. Dip a paintbrush into the water and paint over the crayon marks, if desired.

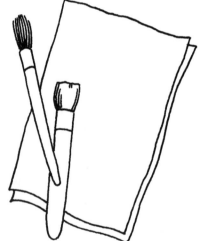

Variations
• Experiment using different textures and colors of paper.
• Make your own paint crayons. Mix dry tempera paint and water to a thick consistency, pour it into a muffin tin, and allow it to dry.

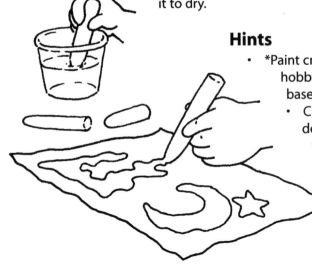

Hints
• *Paint crayons can be found at school supply, art, or hobby stores. They are crayon-shaped, watercolor-based paint.
• Change the water often to make the brightest designs. Encourage artists to change their own water.
• Do not leave paint crayons soaking in the dish of water or they will dissolve and disintegrate.

Candle Crayons

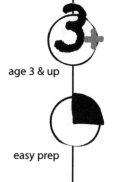

Materials

white paper
candles (all shapes, sizes, and colors)
crayons, optional
water
cup
watercolor paints
paintbrush
iron, optional

Art Process

1. Place a sheet of white paper on the work surface.
2. Draw on the paper using various candles. Press down hard enough to leave visible marks.
3. If desired, use crayons to draw additional designs on the candle drawing.
4. Pour water into a cup (to use as rinse water for the paintbrushes).
5. Paint over the picture with the watercolor paints to reveal your candle drawing. (This is called a wax resist.)
6. The drawing may be wrinkled or curled after it dries. If desired, turn the paper over and iron it with a warm iron (adult only).

Variations

- Write secret messages for a friend to reveal.
- Cover a party table with a large sheet of white butcher paper. Use the candles to draw pictures of a celebration. Then, provide each party guest with a cup of colored water and a paintbrush so they can uncover the secrets on the table.
- Use a wash of thinned tempera paint or ink instead of water-color paints.
- Create a dramatic wax resist by drawing with candles and brightly colored crayons. Then, paint over the drawing with black or dark blue tempera paint.

Hints

- Rinse the paintbrush in the plain water after each color change. Change the water often to maintain the truest colors.
- Press down hard when drawing with the candles.

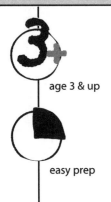

age 3 & up

easy prep

Transparent Crayon

Materials

white paper
crayons
cooking oil
cotton balls

Art Process

1. Place a piece of white paper on the work surface.
2. Draw on the paper with the crayons, pressing down hard as you draw.
3. Pour a small amount of cooking oil on a cotton ball.
4. Rub the cotton ball over the back of the white paper.

Variations

- Use baby oil or mineral oil instead of cooking oil.
- Spread the oil using a paintbrush or cotton swab instead of cotton balls.
- Experiment using different types of paper.

Hint

- Some artists may not like the feeling of or results of oil. Keep in mind that this is normal for young children.

RUB A LITTLE OIL ON THE BACK...

Chalk Dip

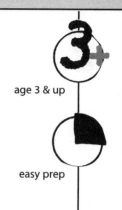

Materials

black or dark paper
measuring spoons
thick, white tempera paint
lid of a jar
colored chalk

Art Process

1. Place a piece of black or dark paper on the work surface.
2. Pour 1 tablespoon (15 ml) of thick, white tempera paint into the lid of a jar.
3. Dip the end of a piece of colored chalk into the tempera paint.
4. Draw on the dark paper with the moist, whitened chalk. The marks will show the distinct color of the chalk, edged with white tempera paint.

Variations

- Make a sampler of markings such as zigzags, spirals, curves, and straight lines.
- Experiment by reversing the colors. Dip the chalk in black paint and draw on white paper.
- Scrub the tempera-dipped chalk on the paper to create a mixed, blurry tint.

Hint

- Chalk can smudge on hands, clothes, and paper.

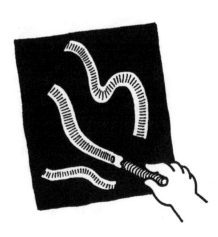

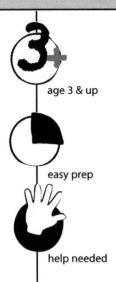

age 3 & up

easy prep

help needed

Cinnamon Drawing

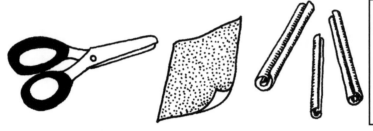

Art Process
1. Cut the sandpaper into shapes or use as is.
2. Use a cinnamon stick to draw on the sandpaper.

Variations
- Make a holiday garland. Cut the sandpaper into holiday shapes, punch holes in them, and string them on a piece of yarn. Place other decorations between each shape, such as Styrofoam peanuts, pieces of foil, pieces of colored paper or wrapping paper, or playdough beads. Hang it in the room and enjoy the fragrance!
- Make a fragrant necklace. Cut out little squares of cinnamon-designed sandpaper, punch holes in them, and string them on a piece of yarn.
- Glue glitter or yarn to the edges of the sandpaper designs.

Hints
- Sandpaper is difficult to cut and can dull scissors.
- Young artists enjoy scribbling and scrubbing the cinnamon on the sandpaper for its fragrance more than for its design.

Baby Oil Drawing

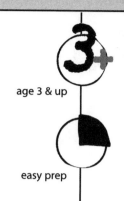

Materials

baby oil
small dish
cotton balls, cotton swabs,
  or a paintbrush
bond paper, any color

Art Process

1. Pour baby oil into a small dish.
2. Dip a cotton ball into the dish of baby oil.
3. Using the oil-soaked cotton ball, draw a design on a piece of paper.
4. Dip other drawing tools, such as a cotton swab or a paintbrush, into the oil and draw on the paper.
5. After the oil has soaked into the paper, hold it up to a light to see the transparent design.

Variations

- Paint a watercolor design over the baby oil drawing and observe how the oil resists the paint.
- Draw a picture with crayons on a piece of paper; then rub an oil-soaked cotton ball over it to enrich the colors.

Hints

- To prevent the dish of baby oil from tipping, tape a loop of wide masking tape to the bottom of it and press it to the table.
- Young artists may use many cotton balls for each drawing as they explore the delightful feel of the soft, oily cotton ball.

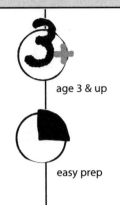

age 3 & up

easy prep

Glossy Pen Paper

Art Process

1. Place a sheet of heavy, glossy paper on the work surface.
2. Draw on the paper with markers. Feel the pens slide and watch the colors glide.
3. If desired, pour water into a cup. Then, dip a paintbrush into it and smudge and blur the pen marks (like "paint-with-water" books).

Variations

- Dampen the paper with a sponge and then draw on the wet, glossy paper.
- Experiment using markers on other unusual types of paper.

Hint

- Printers are valuable sources for free and unusual papers. Ask a local printer to save a box of papers in all colors, textures, and sizes. Visit a print shop and ask for scrap pieces of heavy, glossy paper.

Materials

heavy, glossy paper
markers
paintbrush,
   optional
cup, optional
water, optional

PRINT SHOP
SCRAPS

Fried Paper Plates

age 3 & up

easy prep

help needed

caution

Materials

electric skillet
aluminum foil
old crayon stubs
paper plates
oven mitts
old cheese grater
wooden craft stick

Art Process

1. Line an electric skillet with aluminum foil.
2. Turn on the electric skillet and set it to 150° F or a warm setting.
3. Peel the paper off the old crayons.
4. Place a paper plate on the warm skillet.
5. Grate the crayons and drop the bits and shavings onto the paper plate.
6. Put on oven mitts to protect your hands.
7. Use the end of a wooden craft stick to move the crayon shavings around on the plate.
8. Remove the plate from the skillet when you finish your design.

Variation

• Use a warming tray instead of an electric skillet to melt the crayons.

Hints

• Before placing the paper plate into the skillet, attach a tab of masking tape to a corner of it. Use the tab to remove the plate from the skillet when you finish.
• Place a loop of masking tape on the back of the paper plate before placing it in the skillet to prevent it from moving around.

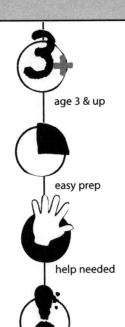

age 3 & up

easy prep

help needed

caution

Sandpaper Melt

WEAR A HEAVY WORK GLOVE...

Materials

electric warming tray
aluminum foil
old crayons
sandpaper, medium grade
thick work gloves

Art Process

1. Cover the electric warming tray with aluminum foil.
2. Turn on the warming tray to a warm setting.
3. Peel the paper off the old crayons.
4. Place a piece of sandpaper on the heated warming tray.
5. Put a thick work glove on your non-drawing hand. Use this hand to hold the sandpaper down.
6. Slowly draw or rub the peeled crayon over the heated sandpaper.
7. Remove the finished design from the warming tray.
8. Allow the drawing to cool and harden.

Variation

• Experiment using other papers, such as drawing or typing paper.

Hints

• Tape the corners of the sandpaper to the warming tray to prevent it from wiggling.
• Place the warming tray on a table against a wall and tape the cord to the table to prevent tripping.
• Use caution with the warming tray. Always supervise projects involving heat!

Fuzzy Glue Drawing

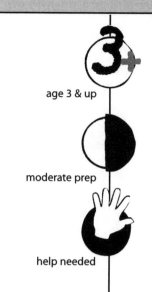

age 3 & up

moderate prep

help needed

Materials
paper plate or matte board
yarn
scissors
plastic bag or plastic container with lid
white glue
small dish
paintbrush

Art Process
1. Place a paper plate or matte board on the work surface. (This will be the "base" of your project.)
2. Wind yarn around your finger about fifteen times. Cut through the end of the loops.
3. Snip the yarn into ½" (1 cm) or smaller pieces and place them into a plastic bag or container. (Cut different lengths or use different colors, if desired.)
4. Pour white glue into a small dish.
5. Dip a paintbrush into the glue and paint over a small area of the base.
6. Choose a color of yarn and pat it onto the glued area.
7. Paint more glue in different areas of the base and pat other colors of yarn into the glue.
8. Make a glue and yarn design, or fill the entire base with yarn.

Variation
• Draw a picture with the glue and use different colors of yarn to create fuzzy yarn pictures.

Hints
• Use colors of yarn that contrast with the color of the base.
• Work on small areas at a time to prevent the glue from drying out too soon.
• The trick to a successful project is to spread the glue on the base and then press the yarn into the glue. Do not dip the yarn into the dish of glue first.
• Offer help with wiping hands and snipping yarn, but the artists should draw and cover the glue pictures themselves.

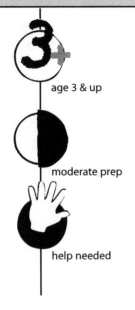

age 3 & up

moderate prep

help needed

Salty Paint Shake

Materials

table salt
powdered tempera paints
empty margarine or yogurt containers
salt shakers
white glue in
   small jars
paintbrushes
paper
tray

Art Process

1. Mix the salt with powdered tempera paint in an empty margarine or yogurt container.
2. Pour the colored salt into a salt shaker.
3. Make additional colors and pour them into other salt shakers.
4. Dip a paintbrush into a jar of white glue. Draw a glue design on a piece of paper.
5. Shake the colored salt onto the glue design.
6. Tilt the paper and shake the excess salt onto a tray. Reuse the excess salt, if desired.

Variation

- Use white beach sand instead of salt. Purchase sand at hardware stores or bring it home from a seashore or a river.

Hints

- Some children have more success squeezing glue out of a glue bottle rather than using a paintbrush.
- For younger children, place about 1" (2 cm) of colored salt into a plastic tub. Place the glue drawing into the tub and let the artist use his or her hands to pour salt on it. This will create a thicker coloration and design.

Fingerprints

Materials

coloring methods (see list)
paper
fine-tip markers

Art Process

1. Choose a coloring method (see list).
2. Color your finger or thumb using the chosen coloring method.
3. Press your colored finger onto a piece of paper. Press several times before re-coloring it.
4. After the fingerprints have dried, use fine-tip markers to add details, such as facial features, hats, cars, or feet.

Variation

- Draw a picture with a crayon and add fingerprints to enhance it. Some examples include fingerprint blossoms in a crayon tree or flowerpot, fingerprint hair on a funny face, or fingerprint bugs on a crayon branch.

Hint

- Some artists enjoy messy hands and fingers; others find the mess almost unbearable. Some of the aversion is due to a developmentally recognized correlation between messy hands and potty training. This aversion usually passes as the artists get older.

Coloring Methods

food coloring—pour liquid into a jar lid and dip fingers in it
markers—draw on the fingertips
ink pads—press fingertips onto the pad
tempera paints—pour paint onto pads of damp paper towels and press fingertips on it

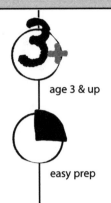

age 3 & up

easy prep

Sponge Chalk

Materials
large, flat sponge
water
colored chalk
paper

Art Process
1. Wet a large, flat sponge.
2. Draw freely on the wet sponge using colored chalk.
3. Press the sponge onto a piece of paper to make a print of the sponge design.

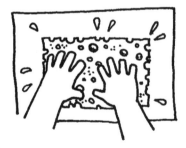

Variation
• Grind, crush, or grate chalk into a dish. Dip a corner of the wet sponge into the chalk and dab it on the paper.

Hint
• Chalk breaks easily, so continue to use the small pieces until they are too small to hold. Save the tiny pieces to grind or crush into powder to use for other art projects.

Negative Space

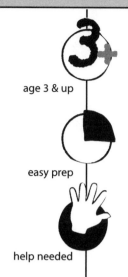

Materials
scissors
large newsprint
paint easel
markers, crayons

Art Process

1. Cut a hole or shape out of a piece of newsprint.
2. Attach the newsprint to the easel.
3. Draw on the paper, using the negative space as part of the drawing.

Variations

- Cut paper into shapes and draw on them.
- Glue a colored shape to newsprint and incorporate it into the drawing.

Hint

- Many artists are uncomfortable having a hole in the middle of their papers. Encourage them to enjoy the negative space.

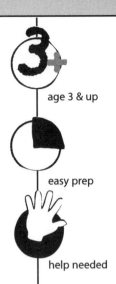

age 3 & up

easy prep

help needed

Crayon Hands

Materials
colored paper
crayons or pencils
scissors
glue
paper scraps

Art Process

1. Place your hands on a piece of paper.
2. Ask a second person to trace your hands on the paper. Or, if you prefer, you may trace your own hands.
3. Cut out the hand shapes.
4. Trace and cut as many hand shapes as desired. Plan your design idea before you begin the project, or let it evolve as you trace your hands. Look at the hand shapes and decide how to use them.
5. Glue the hand shapes to a piece of paper.
6. Decorate your hand shapes by gluing paper scraps to it or drawing on it.

Variations

- Use the hand shapes to make a turkey, ghost, reindeer antlers, cat, chick, duck, bunny, angel wings, tulips, a butterfly, or random hand designs.
- Trace your bare feet and use the cutouts to make designs.
- Make moving parts on your design using brads*.

Hints

- *Brads are thin, flat, small-headed nails.
- Once young artists get the idea of seeing shapes in common objects, such as hands used for deer antlers, they will discover many shapes in all parts of their visual world.

USE EARTH TONES TO MAKE FALL LEAVES!

Tape and Chalk Stencil

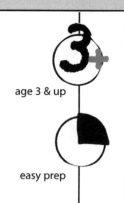
Materials

masking tape
matte board or cardboard
sponge
colored chalk

Art Process

1. Use masking tape to create a design on the matte board or cardboard.
2. Dampen a sponge with water.
3. Rub chalk or draw chalk designs on the damp sponge.
4. Press the sponge all over the taped matte board or cardboard. (The chalk will stick to the paper.)
5. Peel off the masking tape to reveal a stencil design.

Variations

- Use watercolor paint instead of chalk.
- Cut the masking tape into shapes.
- Use clear contact paper instead of masking tape.

Hints

- If you leave the tape on the paper too long, it will not come off.
- To make peeling easier, leave a little edge of tape sticking up.

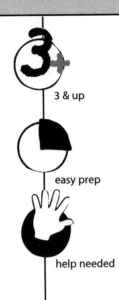

3 & up

easy prep

help needed

Fabric Pen Stencil

Materials

white cotton fabric
such as a shirt,
sheet, pillowcase,
or tablecloth
masking tape
scissors
clear contact paper
fabric pens

Art Process

1. Spread the fabric on a table and tape down the corners.
2. Cut out shapes or designs from clear contact paper.
3. Peel the backings from each shape and press them onto the fabric.
4. Using fabric pens, draw, color, trace, or scribble over the fabric and the contact paper shapes.
5. Peel off the contact paper from the fabric, revealing a stencil design.

Variations

- Cut out letters from the contact paper and spell names or greetings on the fabric.
- Cut out a stencil design from a square of contact paper. Place the square (with the hole) on the fabric and color in the hole to create an opposite effect.
- Stick pieces of tape to heavy paper, color over them, and remove the tape.

Hints

- Fabric pens are available at fabric stores.
- Artists may need help peeling the backing from the contact paper and/or controlling the sticky unruliness of it.
- Artists may need help in understanding the concept of coloring with stencils. Let them practice on small scraps of fabric before using a shirt or pillowcase.

T-SHIRT STRETCHED
OVER CARDBOARD.

PEEL AWAY FOR A
NEGATIVE PATTERN!

Fabric Starched Chalk

Materials

cotton fabric
scissors
liquid starch
bucket or bowl
tray
colored chalk

SOAK FABRIC IN LIQUID STARCH

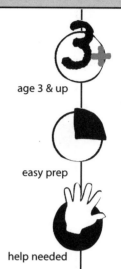

Art Process

1. Cut the cotton fabric into squares.
2. Pour liquid starch into a bucket or bowl.
3. Soak a square of cotton fabric in the liquid starch.
4. Remove the fabric from the starch and wring it out.
5. Place the fabric on a tray and smooth out the wrinkles.
6. Use colored chalk to draw a design on the wet fabric.

SMOOTH OUT WRINKLES

Variations

- Place the fabric over a textured surface and draw on it. The chalk will pick up the design of the texture underneath the fabric.
- Display the finished design in a frame or an embroidery hoop.

Hints

- Starch makes the chalk brighter and helps it stay on the fabric better.
- Do not wash the fabric or the design will wash out.

age 3 & up

moderate prep

help needed

caution

Fabric Transfer

Art Process

1. Place the fabric on a thick pad of newspaper.
2. Using the fabric crayons, draw or color a design on a piece of white paper. (Follow the directions on the fabric crayon box.)
3. Place the drawing face-down on the fabric.
4. Turn on the iron to a warm setting.
5. Press the warm iron on the paper, using a firm, straight ironing motion (supervise closely).
6. Remove the piece of paper. The wax from the paper will be melted onto the fabric.

Variations

- Make individual squares and sew them into a quilt.
- Decorate a bandana, book bag, cloth napkins, tablecloth, or any other fabric.

Hints

- When drawing on the fabric, it is important for artists to press down hard with the crayons.
- Fabric crayons are available at all fabric and craft stores and most art supply stores.
- Fabric crayon drawings will not look like regular crayon drawings, but the transferred design will have bright and true colors.
  - As with any ironing project, an adult should either do the ironing themselves or closely supervise older artists when they iron.

Materials

fabric, such as an old sheet, piece of muslin, T-shirt, or pillowcase
newspaper
fabric crayons
white paper
old iron

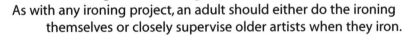

Dot Dots

Materials
paper
drawing or coloring
tools (see list)

Art Process
1. This project explores pointillism, a technique of using nothing but dots to create a larger picture.
2. Place a piece of paper on the work surface.
3. Choose a drawing or coloring tool and create an entire design using only dots of color.
4. Change colors and drawing tools as desired.

Variations
- Combine different art media. For example, use crayon dots for part of the design and paint dots as the background.
- Use contrasting colors, such as green dots on red paper or yellow dots on purple paper.

Hint
- To help young artists understand the approach of Dot Dots drawing, ask them to look through a magnifying glass at the Sunday comics or comic books to see how dots make up the pictures. Or, show them works by pointillism artists such as Seurat.

Drawing or Coloring Tools

crayons
markers
paints and brushes
chalk
oil pastels
colored pencils

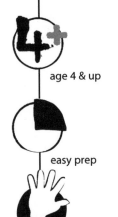

age 4 & up

easy prep

help needed

Peeled Glue

Materials
bottle of white glue
wax paper
markers
thread or yarn,
 optional

Art Process
1. Drip glue onto a piece of wax paper to form a design. Make thick masses, shapes, or forms.
2. Allow the glue to dry until it is hard and clear.
3. Using markers, decorate the dry glue shapes.
4. Carefully peel off the dry, decorated glue shapes from the wax paper.
5. If desired, tie a piece of thread or yarn on the glue shape and hang it from the ceiling. The shapes are great to use as holiday decorations.

Variations
• Make jewelry by threading shapes on a piece of yarn.
• Mix tempera paint into the glue to make colored glue.
• Sprinkle glitter or salt on the glue before it dries to create a sparkling effect.

Hint
• Depending on the weather conditions, it may take several days for the glue to dry.

Baked Stubs

4+
age 4 & up

moderate prep

help needed

caution

Materials
old crayon stubs
cookie sheet
aluminum foil
matte board or
   cardboard
rocks, shells, felt squares,
   pieces of wood, and other items, optional
oven, or a hot, sunny day
craft sticks or coffee stir sticks, optional

Art Process
1. Peel the paper off old, broken crayon stubs.
2. Cover a cookie sheet with aluminum foil.
3. Place a piece of matte board or cardboard on the covered cookie sheet.
4. Randomly place or stack peeled crayons on the matte board.
5. Add rocks, shells, or other items in and around the crayons, if desired.
6. Turn on the oven and set it at 250° F.
7. Place the cookie sheet in the oven for about 10 minutes until the crayons melt (adult only). If it is a hot, sunny day, bring the tray outside and let the sun melt the crayons instead of using an oven.
8. If desired, push the melted crayon around with craft sticks before the melted design cools.
9. Allow the design to cool and remove it from the cookie sheet.

Variation
- Melt crayon stubs on felt squares, fabric scraps, thin boards, cardboard, or other sturdy papers or materials.

Hint
- Make sure the tray is reasonably cool before the artist pokes at the melted crayons.

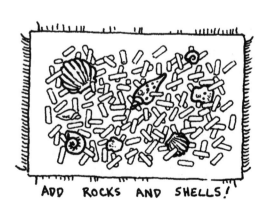

ADD ROCKS AND SHELLS!

age 4 & up

moderate prep

help needed

caution

Layered Color-
Muffins

MELT THE CRAYON
UNTIL LIQUID.

Materials
old crayons
metal cup or small
   pan
aluminum foil
griddle
muffin tin, metal ice
   cube tray, or
   candy mold
oven mitts

THIN LAYERS
OF EACH COLOR...

Art Process

1. Peel the paper off the crayons and separate them by color.
2. Line a metal cup or small pan with aluminum foil.
3. Turn on the griddle to a hot setting. Place the metal cup on the hot griddle and put one color of crayon pieces into it (adult only).
4. When the crayon is melted, pour a thin layer of melted crayon into a muffin tin or mold.
5. Wait for the crayon to cool completely.
6. Choose another color of crayon. Put it in the metal cup and melt it.
7. Pour a thin layer of the second color on top of the first color.
8. Continue to layer colors of melted crayon until the mold is filled.
9. When the crayons are completely cool, pop the Layered Color Muffin out of the mold and use it to color on paper.

CHUNKY STRIPE
CRAYONS!

Hints

- For quicker cooling, put the mold in the freezer.
- Use caution in all the steps involving the heated griddle. Supervise closely!
- To remove paper easily from crayons, soak them overnight.

Squeezy Sandwich Draw

age 4 & up

moderate prep

help needed

edible!

Materials

ketchup, mustard, or spaghetti sauce
squeeze containers
open-faced sandwich, plain bread, English muffin, pizza muffin
ingredients to decorate the sandwich or snack, such as olive slices, tomato
    bits, alfalfa or bean sprouts, sandwich meats, cheese slices,
    and green pepper slices

Art Process

1. Wash hands thoroughly.
2. Make an open-faced sandwich. For example, cover a piece
   of bread with a slice of turkey, then a slice of cheese.
3. Fill squeeze containers with ketchup, mustard, or spaghetti sauce.
4. Draw on the open-faced sandwich with the ketchup or mustard
   squeeze bottle, making a face or other colorful design.
5. Add more decorative food ingredients to finish the design, such as
   alfalfa sprouts for hair, olive slices for eyes, or tomato bits in a pretty
   circle.
6. Make several open-faced sandwiches for friends and family to enjoy!

Variations

- Make a squeezable cheese spread: Grate about 2 cups (250 g) of any
  cheese such as Cheddar or Monterey Jack into a bowl. Mix with 2-3
  tablespoons (40-60 g) of mayonnaise and stir until smooth. If it is too
  thick, add more mayonnaise. Add paprika, salt, pepper, or other favorite
  spices at this time too. Spoon into an empty, clean squeeze container.
  Squeeze to decorate open-faced sandwiches or pizza muffins, or make fancy
  appetizers on carrot slices, celery sticks, or crackers.
- Cover half of an English muffin with a slice of cheese. Fill a squeeze
  container with spaghetti sauce and create a funny pizza face or other
  design. Add bits of other foods to enhance the design.
- Make mini-sandwiches on crackers or slices of narrow French bread.

Hint

- Only add as much ketchup or mustard as would be appetizing! It's easy to
  overdo this part because it's so much fun.

age 4 & up

easy prep

help needed

Lace Rubbing

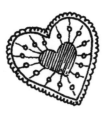  

PLACE TAPE
ON BACK OF
SHAPES...

Materials

scraps of lace
   (fabric or plastic)
scissors
masking tape,
   optional
white drawing
   paper
jumbo crayons

Art Process

1. Cut scraps of lace (fabric or plastic) into shapes such as hearts, squares, or circles.
2. Select a few shapes, place loops of masking tape on them, and stick them to the table.
3. Place a sheet of white paper over the shapes and tape the corners to the table.
4. Peel the paper off the crayons.
5. Rub the peeled crayons back and forth over the paper to reveal the shapes underneath.

Variations

- Move the shapes around, change the colors of the crayons, or cut out new shapes.
- Make greeting cards.
- Cut out shapes and hang them in the window or from the ceiling.
- Substitute paper doilies for lace.

Hint

- Be patient with very young children. They are still learning the idea of rubbings and how to control the crayons.

Texture Table

Materials

textured items
   (see list)
large, light-colored
   butcher paper
masking tape
jumbo crayons

Art Process

1. Spread a variety of textured items over the entire surface of a table. (Make sure the items are fairly flat and not too pointy or sharp.)
2. Place a large sheet of butcher paper over the items, like a tablecloth.
3. Tape the corners and sides of the paper to the table.
4. Peel the paper off the crayons.
5. Using the sides of the peeled crayons, rub them back and forth over the butcher paper to reveal the surprise textures underneath.
6. Press down on the paper to make sure you rubbed all of the textures.
7. Lift the paper and remove the textured items. Leave the butcher paper on the table and use it as a fancy table covering, if desired.

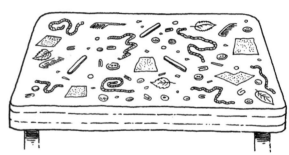

Variations

- Use the paper as a wall decoration or wrapping paper.
- Make small rubbings using a tray and a small sheet of paper.
- Hide items under the paper and ask a friend to rub a crayon over it.

TAPE BUTCHER PAPER SECURELY TO TABLE...

Hint

- Some young artists are still learning the concept of crayon rubbings. With this activity, they can experience rubbings using large arm movements and stable paper.

Textured Items

yarn
paper shapes
coins
glitter
sandpaper
fabric scraps
confetti
paper clips

age 4 up

easy prep

help needed

Glue and Chalk Draw

Materials
white glue, in a
    squeeze bottle
dark paper
colored chalk
hair spray, optional

Art Process

1. Squeeze glue into a design on a piece of dark paper.
2. Allow the glue to dry overnight.
3. Apply colored chalk to the areas between the dried glue lines. The glue lines will appear black and the chalk will have a muted effect on the other areas of the paper.
4. Spray the chalk and glue drawing with a fixative, such as hair spray, if desired (adult only).

Variations

- Draw with the glue on white paper, let it dry, and paint the spaces between the glue lines. The glue lines will appear white.
- Add black India ink to the glue. Draw with the glue on white or black paper, let it dry, and use watercolors or chalk to fill in the spaces.

Hints

- If you use hairspray, spray the artwork outside or in a well-ventilated area.
- The dark paper will dull the chalk, giving it a muted effect.
- Chalk is always messy for young artists, so expect it and enjoy it.

Spider Web

Materials

hammer
nails
3' (1 m) square of
   plywood
heavy string
scissors
paper
chalk
pencils, crayons,
   and markers

Art Process

1. Hammer a nail into the top edge of a plywood square. Be careful not to hammer through the wood into the floor or table.
2. Cut a piece of heavy string, about 2' to 3' (½ to 1 m) long. Tie one end of the string to the nail.
3. Place a sheet of paper in the center of the board.
4. Rub a piece of chalk back and forth over the string, thoroughly coating it.
5. Grasp the loose end of the string and pull it taut over the paper. Using your other hand, lift the center of the string, then let it go so that it snaps against the paper. A puff of chalk will snap against the paper and leave a soft line.
6. Rotate the paper a little. Rub more chalk on the string and snap it to release another line that crosses the first line.
7. Continue turning the paper and snapping chalk lines until the design resembles the framework of a spider web.
8. Move the paper to a table and connect the spider web lines using chalk, pencils, markers, or crayons. Add a spider too, if desired!

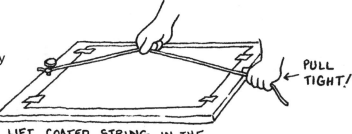

COAT THE STRING WITH CHALK.

Variations

- White chalk on black paper is effective, but try using various colors on white or black paper too.
- Create a design instead of a spider web.

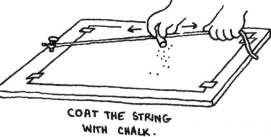

LIFT COATED STRING IN THE CENTER, THEN SNAP ON THE PAPER!

PULL TIGHT!

Hint

- Rubbing chalk back and forth across a string makes it break easily. Continue rubbing the chalk pieces on the string until they get too small to handle. Save the tiny pieces for other art activities.

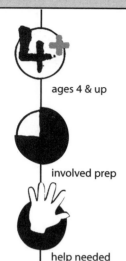

ages 4 & up

involved prep

help needed

Buttermilk Chalk Screen

Art Process

1. Pour buttermilk into a cup.
2. Dip a paintbrush into the buttermilk and paint a piece of paper.
3. Cut a piece of wire mesh screen to fit the old picture frame.
4. Staple the mesh screen to the back the frame.
5. Place the picture frame on the paper so that the screen is not touching the paper.
6. Rub colored chalk back and forth across the screen.
7. Rub different colors of chalk over different areas of the screen.
8. Remove the frame from the paper and watch the chalk absorb the buttermilk on the paper, leaving a sparkling result.

Materials

buttermilk
cup
paintbrush
paper
scissors
wire mesh screen
stapler
old picture frame
colored chalk

Variations

- Repeat the process using paint instead of chalk. Use a nailbrush or toothbrush to spatter paint through the screen.
- Paint over the paper using a mixture of liquid starch and canned milk instead of buttermilk.
- Place paper shapes or stencils on the paper before rubbing the chalk through the screen.

Hints

- Young artists tend to press hard on the screen, so securely attach the screen to the back of the frame. If necessary, reinforce it with duct tape.
- Cover any sharp edges of the screen.
- If you don't have buttermilk, add ½ teaspoon (2.5 ml) vinegar to regular milk and let it sit for 5 minutes. Make sure no one drinks the mixture!

RUB CHALK BACK AND FORTH OVER THE SCREEN.

Stained Glass Melt

age 4 & up

moderate prep

help needed

caution

Materials
old crayons
black, felt-tip markers
white paper
warming tray
heavy glove or oven mitt
scissors and tape, optional

Art Process
1. Peel the paper off the old crayons.
2. Make an outline of a design on a piece of white paper using a black marker.
3. Plug in the warming tray and turn it on.
4. Place the paper on the warming tray (supervise closely).
5. Put a heavy glove or oven mitt on your non-drawing hand. Use this hand to hold down the paper.
6. Color in the design outline using the peeled crayons. Work slowly to allow the crayon to melt and soak into the paper.
7. Remove the design from the warming tray.
8. Hold the paper up to a light or a window to see the stained glass effect.
9. If desired, cut out the design and display it in a window. It will resemble a stained glass window.

GLOSSY STAINED-GLASS EFFECT!

Variations
- For inspiration, look at real stained glass windows.
- Rub the back of the crayon design with a baby oil-soaked cotton ball to make a more transparent design.

Hints
- As with any project involving heat or electricity, observe safety and caution. Tape the warming tray cord to the table and push the table against the wall.
- Some young artists will not understand the concept of stained glass; instead, they will simply enjoy melting crayons into pretty but random designs.

Sandpaper Print

PRESS HARD!

Materials

medium-grade sandpaper
crayons
newspaper
white paper
old iron

Art Process

1. Draw a design on the sandpaper using crayons, pressing down hard as you draw.
2. Place a thick pad of newspaper on the table.
3. Place the sandpaper on the newspaper, drawing side up.
4. Cover the sandpaper with a sheet of white paper.
5. Turn on the iron to a very warm setting.
6. Iron the white paper to melt the crayon marks onto the paper (adult only).
7. If desired, make several prints of the same design. Re-color the design with crayons, place a new sheet of white paper over it, and iron it again.

Hints

- This is a great way for an artist to produce several copies of the same print.
- Some children can do the ironing themselves. If this is the case, work at a low table, tape the sandpaper to the table, and closely supervise them.

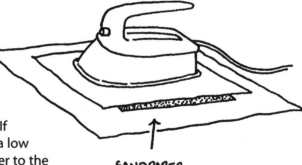

SANDPAPER
IN THE MIDDLE!

Scratchfoam Print

Materials

sheet of scratchfoam or Styrofoam
  grocery tray
scissors
pencil
tempera paint
cookie sheet
brayer (roller) or child's rolling pin
typing paper

Art Process

1. If using a Styrofoam tray, trim off the sides of it.
2. Cut the scratchfoam or Styrofoam into quarters.
3. Using a sharpened pencil, poke holes into the scratchfoam to create a design (see Hints).
4. Pour tempera paint onto a cookie sheet.
5. Roll a brayer through the paint on the cookie sheet.

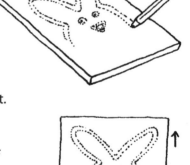

6. Roll the paint-coated brayer across the scratchfoam design.
7. Place a piece of typing paper on top of the scratchfoam and apply gentle pressure with your fingertips.
8. Carefully peel the paper from the scratchfoam.
9. Using the same color, a new color, or several new colors of paint, make another print. Repaint the scratchfoam each time you make a new print.

Variation

- Make several prints of the same design using several different colors of paper. Cut the papers into strips, reassemble the design using different colored strips, and glue the multi-colored design onto a piece of background paper.

Hints

- Any lines or shapes that artists press into the scratchfoam will print white on the white paper; the raised areas of the scratchfoam will print the color of the paint.
- Scratchfoam is available in 9" x 12" (22 cm x 30 cm) sheets at art stores.

RESULTS!

USE GENTLE PRESSURE..

age 4 & up

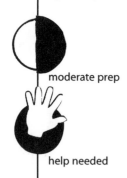

moderate prep

help needed

Little Art Books

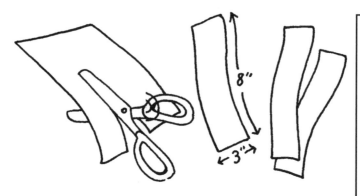

8"

3"

Materials

scissors
lightweight scrap
  paper or
  newsprint
heavy paper
stapler, brads, or
  yarn
crayons or markers

Art Process

1. Cut the lightweight paper into 3" x 8" (6 cm x 20 cm) strips.
2. Fold three or four strips of paper in half.
3. Cut a piece of heavy paper the same size and fold it in half.
4. Place the folded strip of heavy paper around the folded lightweight paper. The heavy paper will be the book cover.
5. Staple together the entire booklet or use some other form of binding.
6. Draw pictures or designs on each page.
7. Decorate the cover.

Variations

- Staple together index cards to make a book.
- Make little art books using different colors of paper.
- Use different types of drawing materials such as colored pencils, stencils, a ruler, and tape.

Hints

- Young artists can make their own books after you show them how to do it.
- Young artists are fascinated by staplers, so be prepared for a substantially stapled creation.
- If the artist has a title for the book, offer to write it on the front cover. Artists may also want to dictate words for adults to write on the pages.

Snowy Etching

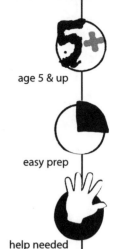

age 5 & up

easy prep

help needed

Materials

crayons
white drawing paper
scraping tool such as a blunt pencil, scissor-
    point, paper clip, or spoon

Art Process

1. Using muscles and determination, completely color a sheet (or section) of white drawing paper. Color hard and shiny, using various shades of blue, white, and gray crayons.
2. Using a black or dark blue crayon, color over the first layer of colors.
3. Scratch a design, such as a snowman, into the top layer of crayon. The first layer of crayon will show through.

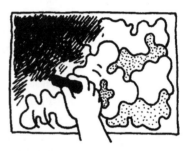

COMPLETELY COVER YOUR FIRST LAYER OF COLORS WITH BLACK OR DARK BLUE.

Variations

· Instead of coloring a second layer of crayon, cover the first layer of crayon with white or black paint. Then, finger paint in the paint. The slick, shiny crayon background makes great finger painting paper.
· Color a square, circle, or other shape in the center of the paper to reduce the challenge of coloring a large area.

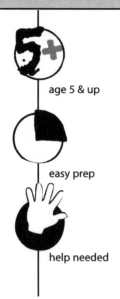

age 5 & up

easy prep

help needed

Crayon-Chalk Transfer

Art Process

1. Cut the matte board or cardboard into a 5" x 5" (13 cm x 13 cm) square.
2. Heavily apply chalk colors to the matte board or cardboard. Cover the entire board or just parts of it.
3. Tap the board to remove excess chalk dust.
4. Color over the chalk colors using the white crayon. (This step requires lots of muscle and determination!)
5. Color over the white crayon with another color crayon. Again, use your muscles and determination.
6. Tape a sheet of smooth paper on top of the matte board.
7. Using a blunt pencil or paintbrush handle, draw a design on the smooth paper (press firmly). The chalk and crayon colors will transfer from the matte board to the bottom of the smooth paper.

Variations

- Experiment using different textures of matte board, colors of paper, and types of chalk.
- Try this project using patterned paper or a dry watercolor painting.

Materials

matte board or
  cardboard
scissors
colored chalk, soft
  type called
  pastels
white crayon
crayon, any color
smooth paper
masking tape
blunt pencil or
  paintbrush
  handle

Hints

- A natural condition of chalk is that it breaks and blurs easily.
- Motivated, energetic artists will enjoy the challenge of all the coloring and covering. Some young artists, however, tire easily or may not be as artistically driven to complete this project.

Chalk Rub

Materials

scrap paper
colored chalk
construction paper, light colors
facial tissues

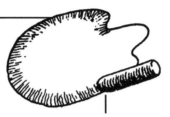

RUB CHALK ON
THE EDGES OF
PAPER SHAPES.

Art Process

1. Tear scrap paper into pieces or shapes.
2. Rub chalk on the edges of the paper shapes.
3. Place a chalked shape on a piece of light-colored construction paper.
4. Use a facial tissue to brush the chalk from the edges of the shape onto the construction paper, creating a blurry-edged stencil.
5. Repeat the process using other shapes.

Hint

- Encourage artists to use only one piece of facial tissue for the entire creation.

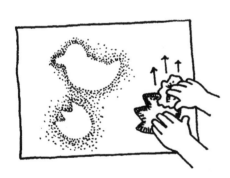

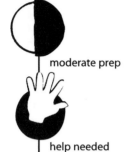

age 5 & up

moderate prep

help needed

Zigzag Gallery

Art Process

1. Cut matte board or poster board into 8" x 10" (20 cm x 25 cm) pieces.
2. Draw a series of pictures or designs on the pieces of matte board. Draw pictures that tell a story, or draw a collection of your thoughts or designs based on one theme.
3. Tape together the drawings so that the pages fold accordion-style.
4. Cut out two pieces of card-board, 8" x 10" (20 cm x 25 cm).
5. Tape the two cardboard covers to the pages of matte board.
6. Fold the zigzag book into a book shape or display the opened gallery on a table or shelf.

Materials

matte board or
   poster board
scissors
crayons or pens
masking tape or
   cloth library tape
cardboard

Variations

- Cut out shapes from paper or wallpaper scraps and paste them to the matte board.
- Illustrate a favorite story or fairy tale.
- Make a zigzag book out of a collection of your artwork, drawings, and designs.

Hints

- This project helps children understand the concept of sequencing.
- Instead of using 8" x 10" (20 cm x 25 cm) pieces, cut the matte board into squares. This will eliminate the possibility of drawings being placed sideways in the finished product.
- Library fabric tape comes in many colors and is available at school supply stores.

Index

Materials Index

50 great ways to explore and create using baking soda, shoe polish, vegetable dyes, and other surprising materials!

Preschool Art
Painting

MaryAnn F. Kohl

Encourage children to experience the joy of exploration and discovery with this new series by award-winning author MaryAnn F. Kohl. Excerpted from the national best-seller **Preschool Art,** each book in the series emphasizes the process of art, not the product. **Preschool Art: Painting** brings you 50 great ways to paint using vegetable dyes, baking soda, cornstarch, shoe polish, and other surprising materials. Make art fun and accessible to children of all ages with these creative, easy-to-do activities!

ISBN 0-87659-224-8 / Gryphon House / 13596 / $7.95

Available at your favorite bookstore, school supply store, or order from Gyphon House at 800.638.0928 or www.gryphonhouse.com.

Preschool Art

50 great ways to explore and create with lace, string, fabric, glue and other easy-to-find materials!

Craft and Construction

MaryAnn F. Kohl

Encourage children to experience the joy of exploration and discovery with this new series by award-winning author MaryAnn F. Kohl. Excerpted from the national best-seller **Preschool Art,** each book in the series emphasizes the process of art, not the product. **Preschool Art: Craft & Construction** gives you 50 great ways to create with lace, string, fabric, glue, and other simple materials. Make art fun and accessible to children of all ages with these creative, easy-to-do activities!

ISBN 0-87659-251-5 / Gryphon House / 19425 / $7.95

50 great ways to explore and create with paper, feathers, buttons, and other easy-to-find materials!

Collage and Paper

MaryAnn F. Kohl

Encourage children to experience the joy of exploration and discovery with this new series by MaryAnn F. Kohl. Excerpted from the national best-sellers **Preschool Art** and **MathArts,** this book emphasizes the process of art, not the product. **Preschool Art: Collage and Paper** gives you 50 great ways to create with paper, feathers, buttons, and other easy-to-find materials. Make art fun and accessible to children of all ages with these creative, easy-to-do activities!

ISBN 0-87659-252-3 / Gryphon House / 15726 / $7.95

Available at your favorite bookstore, school supply store, or order from Gryphon House at 800.638.0928 or www.gryphonhouse.com.